SCHOLASTIC

MATH Word Problems Made Easy

Grade 4

by Bob Krech

NEW YORK • TORONTO • LONDON • AUCKLAND • SYDNEY
MEXICO CITY • NEW DELHI • HONG KONG • BUENOS AIRES

Teaching *Resources*

Dedication

To all the super problem solvers in the
West Windsor-Plainsboro Schools, teachers and students alike

Acknowledgments

Many thanks to Jeff Grabell for his creative
problem contributions

Cover design by Maria Lilja
Interior design by Holly Grundon
Interior illustrations by Mike Moran

ISBN 0-439-52972-7
Copyright © 2005 by Bob Krech
All rights reserved.
Printed in the U.S.A.

5 6 7 8 9 10   40   12 11 10

CONTENTS

Introduction 4

The Fantastic Five-Step Process 6

The Super Seven Strategies 11

  (1) Guess and Check 12

  (2) Draw a Picture 14

  (3) Make an Organized List 16

  (4) Look for a Pattern 18

  (5) Make a Table or Chart 20

  (6) Use Logical Reasoning 22

  (7) Work Backward 24

The Happy Hundred Word Problems 26

  Number and Operations 27

  Measurement 63

  Data Analysis and Probability 68

  Geometry 71

  Algebra 75

Answer Key 77

INTRODUCTION

Problem solving is the first of the process standards listed in the *Principles and Standards for School Mathematics* (NCTM, 2000). Being selected as number one is not surprising in view of this accompanying statement from the National Council of Teachers of Mathematics (NCTM): "*Problem solving should be the central focus of all mathematics instruction and an integral part of all mathematical activity.*" In other words, in mathematics, problem solving is what it's all about.

When learning to read, we learn to recognize the letters of the alphabet, we practice letter–sound relationships, and we learn punctuation; it's all about eventually being able to read text. A similar situation exists in math. We learn how to recognize and write numerals, decipher symbols, determine numerical order, and work with operations like addition and subtraction. But it's all about what we can do with these skills—applying what we know to solve problems in daily life!

Math Word Problems Made Easy: Grade 4 is designed to help you help your students learn more about and increase their problem-solving abilities, and thus their personal math power. This book is divided into three main sections to help you:

The Fantastic Five-Step Process

The first section describes a simple five-step problem-solving process and introductory lesson you can share with your students. This process can be used with every math word problem they might encounter. This is a valuable concept to introduce at the beginning of the year and practice with students so that they will have an approach they can rely on as they encounter various types of problems.

The Super Seven Strategies

In this section, we look at the various types of problems students might encounter and the super seven strategies for approaching them. We discuss each strategy and then provide five sample problems suitable for solving with that strategy. This gives students an opportunity to practice the strategy in a context of math content appropriate to their grade level. You may want to introduce a new strategy every week or so. This way, by the end of the second month of school, students are familiar with all of the basic strategies and have had practice with them.

The Happy Hundred Word Problems

The third section is a collection of 100 math word problems focused on math concepts specific to fourth grade. The problems are written so students will find them fun and interesting (and maybe a little silly). No doubt about it, funny problems focus students' attention. It is much more fun and motivating for students to read about Pierre the Talking Circus Dog as he shops for a hairbrush than it is to consider when the legendary two trains will pass each other.

The problems are arranged by mathematical standard; there are sections of problems for Number and Operations, Measurement, Data Analysis and Probability, Geometry, and Algebra. The individual problems are printed two to a page with a line dividing them, leaving plenty of work space for students to show their thinking. These problems can be used to introduce a concept, practice application of it, or as an end point to check for understanding.

Learning a consistent problem-solving process approach, becoming familiar with and practicing effective problem-solving strategies, and applying these ideas in word-problem contexts help students become more effective problem solvers and mathematicians. And with *Math Word Problems Made Easy: Grade 4*, they can have fun while doing it!

The Fantastic Five-Step Process

What do you do when you first encounter a math word problem? This is what we need to help students deal with. We need to help them develop a process that they can use effectively to solve any type of math word problem.

Word problems often intimidate students because there may be a lot of information; the important facts are embedded in text; and, unlike a regular equation, it is not always clear exactly what you are supposed to do. No matter what type of problem students encounter, these five steps will help them through it. Learning and using the five steps will help students *organize* their interpretation and thinking about the problem. This is the key to good problem solving—organizing for action.

The best way to help students understand the process is to demonstrate using it as you work through a problem on the board or overhead. Make a copy of the graphic organizer on page 7. You can blow this up into a poster or provide each student with his or her own copy to refer back to as you bring students through this introductory lesson.

The Fantastic Five-Step Process

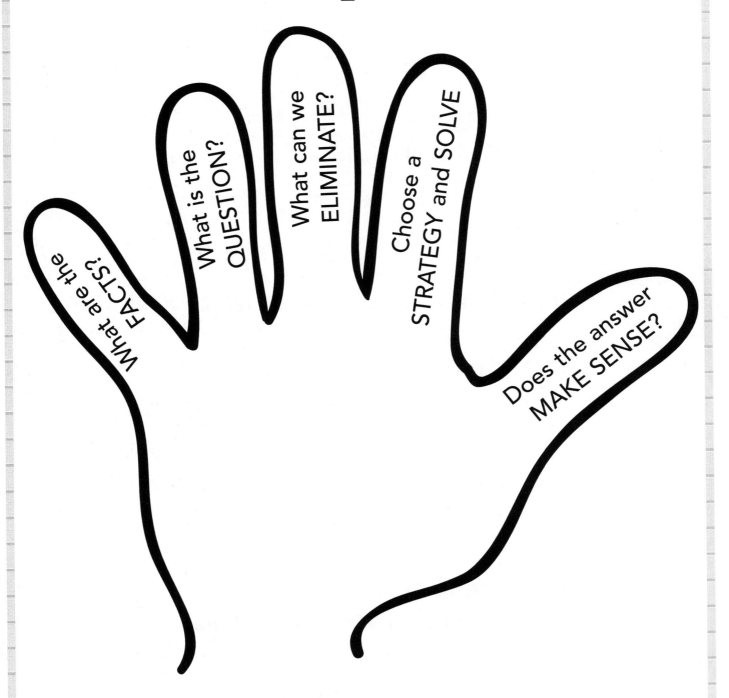

What are the FACTS?

What is the QUESTION?

What can we ELIMINATE?

Choose a STRATEGY and SOLVE

Does the answer MAKE SENSE?

Step 1:
What Do We Know?

Begin by writing this problem on the board or overhead.

> Jock had 72 lima bean-flavored gumdrops in his candy jar. His brother Jack had 89. His sister, Jinx, had 98. Jinx said Jack had more than Jock. Is she right? If so, how many more?

Read the problem carefully. What are the facts? Have students volunteer these orally. Write them on the board.

> Jock had 72 gumdrops.
> Jack had 89 gumdrops.
> Jinx had 98 gumdrops.

Encourage students to write down the facts. This will help them focus on what is important while looking for ways to put it in a more accessible form. Can we arrange the facts in a way that will help us understand the problem situation? For instance, maybe it would be good to draw what we know, or put it in a list, or make a table. Sometimes it's helpful to arrange numbers from lower to higher or higher to lower, especially if we are asked to compare. Are we being asked to compare? Yes!

> Jinx – 98
> Jack – 89
> Jock – 72

Step 2:
What Do We Want to Know?

What is the question in the problem? What are we trying to find out? It is a good idea to have students state the question and also determine how the answer will be labeled. For example, if the answer is 72, then it's 72 what? 72 cats? 72 coins?

We want to know two things:

1. Was Jinx right when she said Jack had more gumdrops than Jock?

2. How many more gumdrops does Jack have than Jock?

Step 3:
What Can We Eliminate?

Once we know what we are trying to find out, we can decide what is unimportant. We may need all the information, but often there is extra information that can be put aside to help focus on the facts.

We can eliminate the fact that Jinx had 98 gumdrops. It's not needed to answer the question. We're left with

Jack – 89
Jock – 72

By comparing the numbers, we can answer the first part of the question now. Jinx was right. Jack has more.

Step 4:
Choose a Strategy or Action and Solve

Is there an action in the story (for example, is something being "taken away" or is something being "shared") that will help us decide on an operation or a way to solve the problem?

Since we have to compare something we have to find the **difference**. Usually the best way is to subtract or add up. This is the action we need to do.

$$\begin{array}{r} 89 \\ -72 \\ \hline 17 \end{array}$$

So Jack had 17 more gumdrops than Jock.

Step 5:
Does Our Answer Make Sense?

Reread the problem. Look at the answer. Is it reasonable? Is it a sensible answer given what we know?

It makes sense for several reasons. For one, 17 is a lower number than the higher number we started with. If it was higher, that would be a problem because the difference between two whole positive numbers cannot be higher than the highest number. Also, if we estimate by rounding, we see that Jack has about 90 gumdrops and Jock has about 70. The difference between 90 and 70 is 20, and 17 is pretty close to that.

Try a number of different word problems using this "talk through" format with students. You can use sample problems from throughout the book. You might invite students to try the problem themselves first and then debrief step-by-step together, sharing solutions along with you to see if all steps were considered and solutions are, in fact, correct. Practicing the process in this way helps make it part of a student's way of thinking mathematically.

The Super Seven Strategies

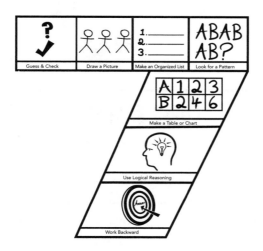

While we should encourage the use of the Five-Step Process to approach any problem, Step 4 (Choose a Strategy or Action and Solve) includes a wide range of choices. Some common strategies that are helpful to teach and practice are listed on the next few pages with sample problems. Students should have experience with all of the strategies. The more practice they have, the easier it will be for them to choose a strategy that fits the problem and helps deliver an answer.

Tip

As students learn about and practice using these strategies to solve problems, ask them to create their own problems. You can list the math concepts you want in the problems (such as addition or money) and even the strategy that must be used to solve it. Students use these parameters to create their own problems, which they can share and try out with one another. As students begin to play with these elements, their knowledge of how problems work grows, as does their confidence when encountering new problems.

Guess & Check

GUESS & CHECK

"**G**uess and Check" means if you're not sure what to do, begin with a reasonable guess to get you started. Look for key words and phrases, like "all together" or "more than," that may help move you in the right direction in choosing an operation. Students should be urged to look at the numbers in the problem and try to apply their estimation skills. This is the key to making a "reasonable" guess. Even just this first step is worth practicing. Then when a first attempted answer is arrived at, consider whether the answer is reasonable, too high, or too low. This is the "Check" part of Guess and Check.

After considering the answer, decide if you need to revise and how. Would a higher answer make sense? A lower answer? A good way to share this strategy with your class is to try one of the following problems on the board and think aloud with them through the steps. Talk out loud as you decide on your first attempt. Explain why you chose that number or numbers. Then talk to them about how you are examining the number to determine if it is reasonable. Talk about how you are adjusting your initial attempt and why.

Answers

1. Norbert is 58 centimeters. Malcolm is 42 centimeters.

2. $140

3. 11 octopi and 3 starfish OR 6 octopi and 11 starfish OR 1 octopus and 19 starfish

4. 3 meters by 3 meters OR 1 meter by 9 meters

5. 17 liters and 11 liters

SAMPLE PROBLEMS

1. Norbert the gnome and his pal Malcolm measure 100 centimeters together. Norbert is 16 centimeters taller than Malcolm. How tall are the gnomes?

2. Lars' pet gila monster, Norton, cost $40 more than Sven's pet peccary, Ralph. Norton cost $180. How much did Ralph cost?

3. Marina is searching the ocean floor for the Prince of Wales. She never found him, but she did see a number of 5-armed starfish and 8-armed octopi. If she saw 103 "arms," how many starfish and octopi could she have seen?

4. Basil the bumbling magician has done it again! Instead of pulling a rabbit out of a hat he pulled out a rather smelly, ill-tempered warthog. For now, he is keeping "Princess" in a cage with a volume of 27 cubic meters. If the sides are in whole meters only and the width is 3 meters, what are possible dimensions for the length and height?

5. Dr. Obvious, the mad scientist, has two bottles of bat sweat on a shelf. Together, the two bottles hold 28 liters. One bottle holds 6 liters more than the other bottle. How much does each bottle hold?

Draw a Picture

DRAW A PICTURE

Drawing a picture can help answer the question in the first step of the problem-solving process: "What do we know?" Sometimes words do not easily convey the facts. Sometimes they can even confuse. By having students draw what they know, the problem can become clearer, and students can arrange and manipulate the facts more easily and discover relationships more quickly.

When students use drawings or diagrams to help solve problems, remind them that they are not creating artwork. Unnecessary details or coloring should be left out. This is also a good occasion to introduce the idea of using simple symbols to represent elements of a word problem, such as a triangle for trees or simple stick figures for people.

Answers

1. 4 slugs

2. 30 pieces of Swiss

3. 36 blocks
(8+7+6+5+4+3+2+1)

4. 80 inches
(6 feet, 8 inches)

5. 4 pizzas

SAMPLE PROBLEMS

1. Slimy Sid's "Fun Bag" holds 10 worms and 6 slugs. How many of which bug would you add to make the probability of picking a slug $\frac{1}{2}$?

2. Charlie Cheddar plans to decorate his birthday cake with a circle of cheese cubes. He has 6 cubes of Gouda and would like to put 5 pieces of Swiss between each piece of Gouda. How many pieces of Swiss does he need?

3. Manfred Mouse fell inside a box of toy blocks. To escape, he needs to build a stairway with the blocks. For Manfred to escape, the stairway must be 8 blocks high. He starts with 8 blocks for the bottom step. For the next step, he lays 7 blocks atop the first set of blocks. If he continues this pattern how many blocks will he need in all to build the stairway?

4. Stupendous Supermarket has agreed to sell Uncle Edsel's Homemade Rhubarb and Clam Pies. Each pie has a radius of 4 inches. If the store decides to display 10 of them in a single row across the top of the bakery counter, how wide will the display be?

5. Myrtle is having 15 guests over for dinner. She plans to serve her scrumptious salamander pizza. If each person (including Myrtle) is expected to eat 2 slices, how many 8-slice pizzas must Myrtle make?

Make an Organized List

1. _____
2. _____
3. _____
_____

MAKE AN ORGANIZED LIST

"**M**ake an Organized List" is a strategy that helps us identify and organize what we know. In problems where, for example, combinations must be determined, listing all possible combinations is essential. Compiling a list can help students see if they have considered all possibilities. Lists, as well as drawings, can also help reveal patterns that may exist.

As an introduction to this strategy it may be helpful for students to use or make manipulatives as they create their lists of data. For example, if you ask students to find all the possible combinations of shorts and T-shirts when you have a red T-shirt, a green T-shirt, a white pair of shorts, and a pink pair of shorts, you might have them use colored cubes to represent the clothes, or color and cut out some simple drawings of the clothes. Students can then list each combination of manipulatives.

Answers

1. 12 outfits

2. 10 games

3. 10 combinations (22 smulps OR 11 smulps and 1 yowch OR 18 smulps and 1 ragus OR 14 smulps and 2 ragus OR 10 smulps and 3 ragus OR 6 smulps and 4 ragus OR 2 smulps and 5 ragus OR 3 smulps, 2 ragus, and 1 yowch OR 7 smulps, 1 ragu, and 1 yowch OR 2 yowch)

4. 5 ways (44 one-foot bars OR 34 one-foot bars and one 10-foot bar OR 24 one-foot bars and 2 10-foot bars OR 14 one-foot bars and 3 10-foot bars OR 4 one-foot bars and 4 10-foot bars)

5. 9 combinations

SAMPLE PROBLEMS

1. Percy the pretentious poodle is selecting an outfit to wear to the Mailman Chaser's Ball. He has 3 collars to choose from (baby blue, forest green, and hot pink) and 4 sets of tags (gold, silver, platinum, and brass). How many different outfits can he make if each outfit is made up of one collar and one tag?

2. The FCHL (Full-Contact Hopscotch League) will begin play next year. Five teams are expected to join the league: Oven Mitt Maulers, Rosebud Raptors, Bambi's Barbarians, Daisy's Destroyers, and The Creampuff Crushers. If each team plays all the others once, how many games will be scheduled?

3. Planet Fez has a unique set of coins. The *smulp* is worth one U.S. cent. The *ragus* is worth 4 U.S. cents, and the *yowch* is worth 11 U.S. cents. Emperor Entar has coins worth 22 U.S. cents in his pocket. How many coin combinations are possible with that amount?

4. Sam Spaniel, the millionaire mutt, has decided to decorate his doghouse. On a recent trip to Doggie Depot, he saw that he could line the front walk of his doghouse with gold bars. After measuring, he discovered he needed 44 feet of gold, which comes in 10-foot and one-foot lengths. How many ways could he order the bars?

5. Renaldo Rat was having a pizza party to celebrate National Rodent Week. Guests could choose very thin, extra thin, or paper-thin crust for their individual pizzas. Topping choices were sunflower seeds, stale cheese, or pickle. How many different combinations of crusts and toppings were possible?

Look for a Pattern

ABAB
AB?
_____

LOOK FOR A PATTERN

Using lists and drawing pictures help reveal patterns that may exist within the information a problem supplies. The guiding question for discovering patterns is, "What relationships do you see between the numbers in the problem?" How far apart are they from each other? Do they increase or decrease by certain amounts in certain ways? Asking these questions will often lead to a good solution.

In a problem where we are told that Surelook lived at 222 Beaker Street and that his next-door neighbor on his left lived at 220, we could use a pattern to tell what the address of the person living on his right, two doors down would be (226). Number lines, hundred charts, and calculators can be useful tools in helping students recognize a pattern that may exist in a problem.

Answers

1. 55 toads

2. 6 rounds

3. 243 chairs

4. 1 hour on Saturday and 1 hour, 40 minutes on Sunday

5. 25 bottles

SAMPLE PROBLEMS

1. A group of toads were planning to set a record and build the biggest amphibian pyramid in history. The plan was to put one toad on the highest level, 2 on the next level, 3 just under them, and so on. In all, the toads hoped that their pyramid would have 10 levels. How many toads would there be in the pyramid?

2. The International Tag Championship will be held next month. 64 teams are scheduled to compete, with each team playing against one other team. The winner of each match goes on to the next round while the loser goes home. How many rounds will it take to crown the champion?

3. Major Morris Minor is setting up the theater for the first of several sold-out bagpipe concerts. The theater has an unusual shape. If Morris puts 3 chairs in the first row, 9 in the second row, 27 in the third row, and 81 in the fourth row, how many chairs will he put in the fifth row?

4. Incredible athlete, Ima Amasing hopes to make the varsity jacks team this year. She practices every day. Here are her training times for the week:

Monday: 40 minutes	Wednesday: 1 hour	Friday: 1 hour, 20 minutes
Tuesday: 20 minutes	Thursday: 40 minutes	

If she continues to follow this pattern, how long will she practice on Saturday and Sunday?

5. Sheldon discovered a new health drink, Slime Tonic, while working in his laboratory. On Monday he brewed one bottle of tonic. On Tuesday, he brewed 4 bottles; on Wednesday, he brewed 9; and on Thursday, he brewed 16. How many bottles did he brew on Friday?

STRATEGY 5:
Make a Table or Chart

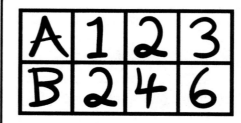

MAKE A TABLE OR CHART

Here's another strategy that helps organize information and thus better answer the first question in the problem-solving process: "What do we know?" Tables or charts are a way to organize two groups of data to better see what the relationship between the two groups might be. It helps make patterns and functions that create patterns more apparent.

For example, if we know that one can of beans costs 5¢, 2 cans are 10¢, and 3 cans are 15¢, by creating a table with this information, students will be able to figure out how much 8 cans of beans would cost *(40¢)*. The table organizes the quantity and the cost so it's easier to see the relationship. As students use tables and charts, caution them as to how far to extend the data. In the case of the problem above, all we need to know is how much 8 cans cost. It wouldn't make sense to extend the table to 10 cans because that would be adding extra work and more information than we need.

Answers

1. 12:10 P.M. (Note: There is no rest period needed after the last event.)
2. 64 kg
3. 6 packages
4. 190 students
5. 4 feet

SAMPLE PROBLEMS

1. The Biannual Goofy Games are holding four events: Anchovy Eating, Liver Juggling, Giant Squid Wrestling, and Porcupine Tag. Each event takes 40 minutes, followed by a 25-minute rest period. You think you have a chance to win all four events! If Anchovy Eating begins at 8:15 A.M., when will you be finished with the competition?

2. Yetta was experimenting in her laboratory, when she created the amazing expanding amoeba. When it was first created, the amoeba weighed 2 kg. When it was one day old, it weighed 4 kg. After the second day it weighed 8 kg. It ballooned to 16 kg after the third day. If the pattern holds, how much will the amoeba weigh after the fifth day?

3. Anchovy cupcakes come three to a package:

Number of Packages	1	2	3	4	5
Number of Cupcakes	3	6	9		

How many packages must be purchased to enjoy 18 cupcakes?

4. Students at Remora Eel Elementary were asked to pick their favorite band. The results are at right. If 500 students were asked the same question, how many would probably pick The Electric Mangoes?

The Lunchroom Blues Band   17
Dog Sweater   14
The Electric Mangoes   19

5. Angus, the lead triangle player with the rock group The Obtuse Angle, thrills the crowd when he jumps off the tallest speaker onto a rubber stage. Each bounce is half the height of the previous bounce. If the speaker is 64 feet off the ground, how high will he bounce after the fourth time he hits the stage?

STRATEGY 6:
Use Logical Reasoning

Logical reasoning is an approach that organizes and analyzes information so that it ultimately leads to a conclusion. Ideas that help students think logically include using lists, pictures, tables, charts, and looking for patterns. A logic matrix and Venn diagram are also helpful tools in organizing information in a logical way and seeing possibilities.

A logic matrix can help us organize facts and use the process of elimination to arrive at an answer. For example, "Jim lives in a blue house and drinks milk. Bert does not live in a green house. The person in the white house drinks juice. Joan drinks water. Where does Bert live?"

Person	House	Drink
Bert		Juice
Joan	Green	Water
Jim	Blue	Milk

Venn diagrams are also very useful for organizing information and supporting logical reasoning. For example, "The Eatalotsky family hosted Thanksgiving. There was a choice of main courses: turkey, ham, or both. Seven of the family members had turkey. Seven had ham. Since there are ten Eatalotskys, how many had both ham and turkey?" The Venn diagram helps provide an answer.

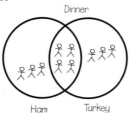

USE LOGICAL REASONING

Answers

1. Bosco – 3rd floor
   Roz – 4th floor
   Ermin – 6th floor
   Siz – 10th floor

2. 8 sides; octagon

3. Blorg, Zatz, Peebleprax, and Klutz

4. 165 pieces

5. Lizard tongue for invisibility; eye of newt for shrinking; batwing turns an enemy to stone; and wolfbane causes sleepiness.

SAMPLE PROBLEMS

1. There is a hyper-speed elevator in the brand-new Kookie Kola Koporate Headkwarters Building. Going up it stops at the 3rd, 4th, 6th, and 10th floors. Each of four people gets off at a different floor. Bosco exits and says goodbye to Ermin. Siz is the last person to get off. Roz gets off one floor after Bosco. At which floor does each person get off?

2. Alma, Cornelia, and Hazel have just purchased the hottest new fashion accessory, Polygon Purses! Alma's purse has 2 more sides than Cornelia's and 3 less than Hazel's. If Cornelia's purse is shaped like a triangle, how many sides does Hazel's purse have? (Bonus: What is the shape of Hazel's purse?)

3. Alien explorers Blorg, Zatz, Klutz, and Peebleprax are standing in a row on the command deck of the *Starship Bigsurprise*. Klutz is not next to either Zatz or Blorg. Blorg is farthest to the left. Zatz stands next to Blorg. Starting from the left, how are the four explorers arranged?

4. The number of pieces of gum in Gussie's used chewing-gum collection is so secret, even she forgot how many there are. She does remember that the number of pieces is an odd number that is more than 100 and less than 200. The number is a multiple of 3 and 5. The sum of the digits in the hundreds and tens places equals 7. How many pieces does Gussie have in her collection?

5. Apprentice Wizard Walter can't remember which ingredient goes with witch (ha ha) spell. He found an ancient parchment with clues. Wolfbane is not used to turn an enemy to stone. Lizard tongue is used for invisibility. Batwing is not used for shrinking. Eye of newt is not used to cause sleepiness or to turn an enemy to stone. Which ingredient goes with which spell?

Work Backward

WORK BACKWARD

Working backward is a good strategy to employ when we know how a problem ends up, but we don't know how it started. For example, if I went to the store and bought a hammer for $2.50 and the clerk gave me $2.50 change, how much money did I give the clerk to begin with? It is still a matter of applying the Five-Step Process and organizing information first, but the trick here is to know where to begin and to think about using inverse operations.

These types of problems are a great opportunity to help students see the usefulness of using letters or symbols to represent unknown quantities. For example, with the hammer problem we could think:

> *I gave the clerk x. And since I got back $2.50 and the hammer costs $2.50, then $2.50 + $2.50 = x.*
> *x = $5.00*

Answers

1. 40 jelly beans
2. 13 centimeters
3. 7 hours
4. 120 pounds
5. $10

SAMPLE PROBLEMS

1. Mitzi bought the jumbo pack of mustard-flavored jelly beans. She gave $\frac{1}{2}$ of the pack to her sister, Messy. Then she gave half of what was left to her other sister, Mossy. After that, she had 10 left to enjoy herself. How many jelly beans were in the original pack?

2. Fleeza knitted 37 shell sweaters for her pet snails. If she used 481 cm of yarn in total and used the same amount of yarn for each sweater, how much yarn was used for each sweater?

3. Ike Iguana entered a fly-eating contest. If he ate a total of 1,820 flies and ate an average (mean) of 260 flies per hour, how long did the contest last?

4. When Adlai makes his Seafood Surprise, he likes to mix 4 pounds of sea urchin for every 3 pounds of kelp. If he made 280 pounds of Seafood Surprise, how many pounds of kelp did he use?

5. Osgood makes $80 per week at his job as an inspector at the dirt factory. He uses his entire paycheck for food, rent, and treats for his pet squirrel Sparky. If he spends $50 for rent and $\frac{1}{4}$ of his paycheck for food, how much is left to buy treats for Sparky?

The Happy Hundred Word Problems

100

The "Happy Hundred Word Problems" are organized by the NCTM content standards. Within each standard section, problems are further organized and labeled by the major math concepts typically found in second-grade math curriculums. For example, Number and Operations is a large standard that includes concepts like place value, money, addition, and subtraction. There are specific word problems here for each of these concepts. The concept focus is marked in the upper left-hand corner of each problem. The answers are provided in the answer key on pp. 77–79.

As you introduce a problem, remind students to use the Five-Step Process. Keep the graphic organizer prominently displayed on a poster or chart, or give students a copy of their own to refer to. On each page you will find two problems with space for students to show their thinking. Encourage students to write down their solution process including any words, numbers, pictures, diagrams, or tables they use. This helps students with their thinking and understanding of the problem, while giving you more assessment information.

When assessing students' work on word problems, two major aspects need consideration: process and product. Observe students as they work on or discuss problems. Focus on what they say, and whether they use manipulatives, pictures, computation on scrap paper, or other strategies. When looking at their written products consider what skills they are exhibiting as well as what errors or misunderstandings they may be showing. This is why it is essential that students "show their thinking" as they solve a problem and explain their rationale.

Finally, have fun! These problems are designed to appeal to kids' sense of humor. Enjoy the situations and the process. Using what they know to solve word problems gives students a sense of mastery, accomplishment, meaning, and math power!

Place Value Through Ten Thousands

The New York Yaks played their first four games this season on the road. Here's their schedule:

Sept. 9	Skunkfoot Stadium	85,000 seats
Sept. 12	Bigtoe Auditorium	55,500 seats
Sept. 19	New Old Theater	20,500 seats
Sept. 27	Ragweed Park	71,000 seats

One of the games drew 72,000 fans. Where was it played?

Place Value Through Hundred Thousands

50,000 glow-in-the-dark nose rings were sold at the first Boogaloo Banshee Band concert. Every time the band gave a concert, the total number of nose rings sold doubled. They gave 4 concerts on their "Summer Home Some Aren't" tour. How many nose rings did they sell at the 4th concert?

Comparing and Ordering Numbers

Biff, Farnsworth, and Harry are in the finals of the Flying Frozen Pizza competition. You have to throw a frozen pizza through a hula hoop from 20 yards away. Everyone has thrown three times except Harry. He has scored 70 and 11 points on his first two throws. Biff has scored 40, 55, and 2 points on his throws. Farnsworth has scored 23, 23, and 40 points. How many points does Harry need to win?

Rounding Numbers

Marilyn Moviestar expects 2,735 guests at her wedding next week. She wants to give each guest a souvenir toaster. The toasters are sold in boxes of 550. How many boxes should she order?

5 Rounding Numbers

Champion pickle thrower Gary Gherkin scored a total of 1,192 points during his matches in November. In December he scored 1,185. In January it was 1,219. Investigative reporter, Iwana Noe wanted to know about how many points Bill scores in a month, to the nearest hundred. What would you tell her?

6 Place Value Through Hundred Millions

Jenna Genius was on the Very Brilliant Kids Quiz Show. She was the given the digits 1, 2, 3, 4, 5, 6, 7, 8, and 9. She was asked to make the largest number she possibly could using each digit only once and write the number using numbers and words. What should she write?

Comparing and Ordering Greater Numbers

Mack, Mick, Mika, and Moki are pinball wizards and avid bike riders. Their pinball tournament scores are awesome. Mack has a red bike. The player with the blue bike scored 85,417,363. Mick scored 85,407,363 and has a purple bike. A player with a bike that is neither blue nor green scored 85,500,001. Moki scored 85,407,363 and has a green bike. Mack claimed he was the winner. Was he right?

Rounding Greater Numbers

Talk about big collections! Yigzat from Planet Flop collects dust specks. She has 11,347,999 specks. Her brother, Bassinet, asked her about how many dust specks she has. What would be her best answer to the nearest million?

9 Comparing Money Amounts

Chuck delivers *The Daily Blab* in his neighborhood. It is collection day on Chuck's paper route. He got a $10 bill, a $1 bill, and a nickel from Mr. Yawn. He got a $5 bill, two $1 bills, and 4 quarters from Mrs. Yap. He got two $5 bills and a half-dollar from Ms. Yelp. Who paid Chuck the most money? How much?

10 Making Change

Silly Sandy arrived at the costume shop at exactly 5:47 P.M. Any costumes bought before 6:00 P.M. were an extra $5 off the marked price. She decided to buy a giant hamster costume for Halloween. The price on the tag was $16.88. She gave the clerk a $20 bill. What's the least amount of coins and bills the clerk could give her in change?

11 Making Change (Reverse)

Pierre the talking circus dog went shopping. He bought himself a grooming brush. It cost $1.35. The clerk gave him three $1 bills, a half-dollar, a dime, and a nickel in change. Pierre said, "Wait. Is that the right change?" The clerk held up the bill that Pierre had given her. Pierre said, "Oh, yeah. That's right." What bill did the clerk hold up? How do you know?

12 Adding With More Than Two Addends

Natasha Noodlenova was looking over the exotic pasta display at the fair. There were 789 noodles from Upper Volta, 210 from Egypt, 99 from Venezuela, 101 from Uruguay, and 25 from Uganda. How many noodles were there from countries that start with "U"?

13   Commutative Property of Addition

Dr. Finkenstein was looking over the registrations for his summer camp. He saw that 57 girls signed up for flaming archery while only 32 boys signed up. On the sign-up for super-ball ping-pong, 57 boys signed up, but only 32 girls. How many children signed up for archery? How many children signed up for ping-pong?

14   Associative Property of Addition

Count Factula set up a summer camp, too. He had 38 girls sign up for sneaker weaving. 95 boys signed up also. 50 children signed up for snakeball. Meanwhile, at Mr. Hyden's camp, 95 boys signed up for centipede catching, while 50 girls did the same. 38 children signed up for worm digging. How many children signed up for Count Factula's camp? How many signed up for Mr. Hyden's camp?

15 Adding Whole Numbers

A great new book called *Stink, Stank, Stunk: The Story of a Skunk*, was just released in Snailsville and sold 80,000 copies on the first day. There are only two bookstores in Snailsville. Barns and Global sold 50,000 more copies than Binky's Books. How many copies did Binky's Books sell?

16 Adding Whole Numbers

This is a bit of a sticky problem. Professor Snort found 21,295 pieces of gum stuck to the bottom of the desks at King Kong College. Professor Snark found 17,545 pieces of gum stuck to the bottom of the desks at Godzilla University. How many pieces of gum did they find all together?

17 Subtracting Whole Numbers

Whistling Willie started his concert trip across the country with 7,895 souvenir whistles to give away to his fans. Along the way he gave out 3,847 whistles. The concerts were so bad, his fans threw 2,001 of the whistles back at him. How many whistles did Willy have at the end of the trip?

18 Subtracting Whole Numbers

The Crack Me Up, Inc. catalog sales results have just come out. They sold 42,395 clown noses, 9,456 crazy wigs, 1,005 sets of wax teeth, and 899 squirt rings. How many more crazy wigs were sold than squirt rings?

19 Estimating Sums and Differences

A bear wandered out of the woods with only $5.75. He went to Pizza Palace where he saw that a personal pan pizza was $3.89 and a large root beer was $1.49. This is what he wanted for lunch. Round the prices to the nearest ten cents and estimate if the bear has enough money to buy his lunch. Does he? Why or why not?

20 Estimating Sums and Differences

Marvelous Mitzi has 377 Ookie-Man cards. She gives her friends 209 of them. Estimate to the nearest ten about how many she has left.

21 ⟩ **Subtracting Across Zeros**

Bizbo from Planet Wowee is trying to save
enough gizzies to buy a space bike that costs
7,000 gizzies. So far he has 5,490 gizzies. "I'm
never going to save enough," he moaned to
his sister, Bazba.

Bazba did a quick calculation and said,
"Don't worry, you're not that far off." How
many more gizzies does Bizbo need?

22 ⟩ **Using Doubles to Multiply**

Boris Bookworm just bought
bookcases for his room. Each
bookcase has 4 shelves and
can hold 8 books on a shelf.
He has 4 bookcases in the
room and they are filled. How
many books does Boris have
in his room?

23 Multiplication

Liza Legume earned $4.00 for every hour she baby-sat Little Sweetums. She baby-sat on Monday, Tuesday, and Wednesday for 3 hours each day. She baby-sat on Saturday, Sunday, Thursday, and Friday for 2 hours each day. How much money did she earn baby-sitting for the week?

24 Commutative Property of Multiplication

Rodney Rockwell was displaying his rock collection at the big "Rock On!" rock show. He put them out in 8 rows with 9 rocks in each row. His arch rival in the rock show business, Nestor Newrock, wanted his collection to look better. He put out 9 rows with 8 rocks in each row. Who had the most rocks on display? Write multiplication sentences to describe each boy's collection.

25   Multiplication: Property of One

Since 1921, Old Smelly, the unusual geyser, has been erupting once a year. In even-numbered years, it sprays water in the air for 121 minutes when it erupts. In odd-numbered years, the spray goes on for twice as long as in even-numbered years. How many minutes did Old Smelly spray in 1980?

26   Associative Property of Multiplication

The fourth-grade classes in Yipee Elementary School were collecting empty cereal boxes to help their art teacher, Paula Picasso, create a cereal-box sculpture. Mrs. X's class handed in 3 shopping bags with 2 boxes in each bag. Mrs. Y's class handed in 3 shopping bags with 2 boxes in each bag. So did Mrs. Z's and Mr. Q's. How many cereal boxes were collected?

27 Using Patterns to Multiply

It's time for the Annual Yipee Elementary School picnic. Last year, 109 students came to the picnic. This year, 26 fewer students are coming, but each one wants a hot dog. Principal Tasty is ordering the hot dogs. He ordered 10 packs. There are 9 hot dogs in a pack. Will there be enough? How do you know?

28 Relating Multiplication and Division

Twenty-seven players signed up for Doctor Dunkenstein's Three-On-Three Invitational Ratball Tournament. Dr. D. has to set up the teams. How many teams will he have? What multiplication fact can help you find the answer?

29 · **Using Doubles to Divide**

Tania Twinster is packing gift boxes of her famous beetle brittle candy. She puts 2 pieces in each little gift box. She has 48 pieces of candy. How many gift boxes does she need?

30 · **Division Without Remainders**

Fierce Fred's gang is trying to make an escape across the Raucous River. There are 40 ferocious fellas in Fred's gang. There are 8 escape boats at the edge of the river. Fred wants the same number of fellas in each boat. How many fellas should get in each boat?

31   **Division Without Remainders**

Mrs. Shifty bought a pack of 72 stickers. There are 30 students in her class. She is going to give one sticker to each of her art students who completed the extra-credit assignment of building a full-sized replica of the Eiffel Tower with toothpicks. Only 9 students did the extra credit. Mrs. Shifty wants to give out all the stickers. How many should each student get?

32   **Division Without Remainders**

Everyone in Mr. Dramatic's new play, *The Sad Little Salt Shaker*, is getting a costume today. Each person must wear 5 scarves as part of the costume. 45 scarves were given out by the prop department. There are 15 people in the play. How many people did not get their scarves?

33 Division With Remainders

It took the Intergalactic Space Commandos 25 days to round up 31 loose asteroids. Asteroid container ships can hold 6 asteroids each. At least how many container ships do they need?

34 Division With Remainders

Buffalo Benny is preparing for some trick shooting. He has 75 pebbles. Each one of his trick slingshots holds 9 pebbles. He wants to load up his slingshots and put any extra pebbles in his pocket. How many slingshots should he load up? How many extra pebbles will go in his pocket?

35   Multiples of 10, 100, 1,000

Sheila Surefoot is climbing mountains this summer to earn her mountain-climber merit badge. She climbed to the top of 4 mountains, each with a height of 400 feet. To earn the merit badge she must climb a total of 1,400 feet. Did she earn the merit badge? Why or why not?

36   Multiples of 10, 100, 1,000

"720 Lost Fruitcakes Recovered From Loopy Lagoon!" screamed the headline in *Nonsense Weekly*. The fruitcakes were packed in boxes with 80 in a box. How many boxes were pulled up?

37 — Multiples of 10, 100, 1,000

"Yahoo! $8,000 for each of us!" yelled Mr. Rutabaga. He got off the phone and danced. He had just won a radio trivia contest that awarded $8,000 to each member in his family. He told his wife, Marigold, his sons, Ollie and Jollie, and his daughter, Malicious. They danced, too. How much money did Mr. Rutabaga win?

38 — Multiplying Two-Digit Numbers by One-Digit Numbers

The Pomegranate Sisters love to run in an unusual way—backwards on their tiptoes. Penelope ran 7 miles a day for 12 days. Pineapple ran 6 miles a day for 13 days. Periwinkle ran 9 miles a day for 8 days. Who ran the most miles?

39 Multiplying Two-Digit Numbers by One-Digit Numbers

Business is booming at Bodacious Bernie's Bust-Yer-Gut Bakery. The bakery opened Saturday morning at 7:00 A.M. In the first 2 minutes, 6 customers each bought a dozen doughnuts. In the next 3 minutes, the same thing happened. How many doughnuts were sold in the first 5 minutes?

40 Estimating Products

Herman watches a lot of TV. In fact, he watched 49 minutes of TV every day for a week. His cousin, Snodgrass, watches even more. He watched 3 times as much as Herman watched. Estimate about how many minutes of TV Snodgrass watched in a week.

41 Multiplying Three-Digit Numbers by One-Digit Numbers

The Tofu Triplets, Tony, Tangelo, and Tornado, like to work together but are very picky about everything being equal. They weeded their yard and counted the weeds to make sure they each did the exact same amount of work. Each boy picked 214 weeds. How many weeds did they pick all together?

42 Multiplying Four-Digit Numbers by One-Digit Numbers

"Each one of these bags has 1,293 bottle caps in it," the salesman said.

"I'll take 8 bags," Flip replied. "I'm going to need at least 9,000 caps to cover the walls of my room."

"Wait," said the salesman. "I'll sell you another bag for half price." Does Flip need the extra bag?

 **Multiplying Two-Digit Numbers**

Thirteen guests are coming to Sally Sugar's Sweet Sixteen Party. She is giving each of them 16 silver staples. A box of silver staples costs $.70. There are 10 staples in a box. How much will it cost Sally to buy silver staples for all of her guests?

 **Multiplying Two-Digit Numbers**

Consistent Connie gets a score of 89 every time she goes bowling. Last year Connie bowled 3 times a month. What was her total score for the year?

45 — Multiplying Three-Digit Numbers by Two-Digit Numbers

Hermione Hedgehog does a lot of walking even though she is 113 years old. Her neighbor, Ethel Emu also walks a lot, though she is 119. Hermione walks 135 miles every two months. Ethel walks 47 miles every month. Who walks the most in a year?

46 — One-Digit Divisors With Money

"Mom gave me $18 to split evenly among the 3 of us," said Penelope.

"Excellent! I'm going to use my share to see that new movie, *The Turtle That Ate Tokyo!*" exclaimed Portia.

"Tickets are $7.00," said Patience. "Are you sure you'll have enough?"

"Of course," said Portia. Do you agree with Portia? Why or why not?

47 Two-Digit Quotients With and Without Remainders

Dastardly Dan had stolen 68 bicycles when he was finally caught. He was ordered by the judge to give an even amount of bikes to each of the 3 biking clubs in town. Any extras would go to the police for their bike patrol. How many bikes did each club get? Did the police get any? If so, how many?

48 Regrouping in Division

"Only 6 days left in the school year," lamented Mrs. Locker. "And I still have 74 pages of math for the kids to do. I'll have to assign them the same number of pages each day that's left. Any extra pages, they can do during their summer vacation." How many pages of math will she give her class each day during the rest of the school year? How many pages will they have to do during summer vacation?

49 — Dividing Multiples of 10, 100, and 1,000

One hundred and fifty Badminton All-Star Collector Cards were in the old trunk being auctioned on "e-boy." Bill, Baldy, and Bingo chipped in to buy it online. They decided they would split it 3 ways. How many cards should each boy get?

50 — Three-Digit Quotients

"There are 992 planets to be explored in Solar System X," stated Space Commander Galactica. "We have 8 explorer craft ready. Each craft will explore the same number of planets." How many planets did Galactica assign to each explorer craft?

51 **Dividing Money**

Cecilia Coffeecup paid $5.60 for 5 cups of coffee at the Java Joint. She was given 40 cents change after paying with six $1 bills. How much does a cup of coffee cost at the Java Joint?

52 **Dividing with Zeros in the Quotient**

Determined Donald scored 832 points playing his new electronic game, Nonetendo. He played 4 games and scored the same amount of points in each game. How many points did he score in a game?

53 Finding Averages

Ringo loves playing horseshoes. He played 4 games. In the first game he got 8 ringers. In the second game he got 3 ringers. In the third game he got 4 ringers and in the fourth game he got 5 ringers. What is the average number of ringers for Ringo?

54 Finding Averages

So far Professor Pointy's Puppet Show, *The History of Melons*, has been open for four shows. The professor wrote down the number of tickets sold at each show.

M	T	W	Th
50	25	15	10

What is the average number of tickets sold for one of the professor's puppet shows?

55   **Dividing Greater Numbers**

12,440 free marshmallows are being given out at the Annual Monkeyville Marshmallow Celebration. There are 8 welcome stands where the marshmallows are given out. Mel Oh is putting the same number of marshmallows at each station and eating any extras. How many marshmallows did he put at each station? Did he eat any extras? If so, how many?

56   **Representing Fractions**

There are 12 players on the Gallivanting Gophers shoe tossing team. 4 of the players are under 12 years old. One player is 13. The rest are 12 years old. What fraction of the team is 12 years old?

57   Fractional Parts of a Number

Mr. Corkboard teaches fourth grade. There are 21 students in his class. Two-thirds of his class brought their lunch on Friday. The rest of the class ordered pizza yogurt. Pizza yogurt costs 2 lunch tickets. How many lunch tickets should Mr. Corkboard send down to the cafeteria?

58   Equivalent Fractions

Jimmy and Jimmie are twins. They are in different fourth-grade classes. Each class has 24 students in it.

Jimmy said, "My class is $\frac{3}{4}$ boys."

Jimmie replied, "Well, my class is $\frac{12}{16}$ boys." Which class had more boys?

Fractions in Simplest Form

Petunia found an old pirate recipe for making punch. It said that she needed $\frac{12}{18}$ of a cup of jungle juice. "My measuring cup isn't marked in eighteenths," she lamented. "It only has thirds, halves, and quarters." Can she still use it to measure the jungle juice? How?

Comparing and Ordering Fractions

Big Boss Billy had his crews out painting dog houses. The houses were the same size and right next to each other. By the end of the day Crew #1 finished $\frac{2}{3}$ of Fido's house. Crew #2 had finished $\frac{4}{12}$ of Fifi's house. Which crew got the most painting done? How do you know?

61 Improper Fractions and Mixed Numbers

Cassandra Cookenough was making her well-known (and deeply dreaded) asparagus waffles for the big family holiday breakfast. She would make a waffle and then cut it into quarters. Each quarter was a serving. Her boyfriend, Egon Eatalot, wanted to show her how much he loved her cooking so he ate 11 servings. How many waffles did he eat?

62 Adding With Like Denominators

Mrs. Tiremeout said she would buy her class the black cloth they needed to make the giant squid costume for Halloween. They split the measuring between two groups. The first group needed $\frac{3}{8}$ of a yard of cloth. The second group needed $\frac{4}{8}$ of a yard of cloth. How many yards of cloth should Mrs. Tiremeout buy?

Subtracting With Like Denominators

Cornelius Crumbbun found a treasure. It consisted of 6 gold bricks and $\frac{9}{10}$ of another gold brick. Cornelius said, "I think I'll give my nephew, Little Crumby, 4 gold bricks and $\frac{4}{10}$ of another." How much gold will Cornelius have left?

Fractions and Decimals

"I'll give you a choice," said Smart Aleck to his little brother, Smart Alan. "You can have $\frac{7}{10}$ of a dollar or $0.75." Which amount should Smart Alan choose? Why?

Decimals

"This Giganto Chocolate Bar can be cut into 200 pieces," said Carl Candyman. "How much do you want?"

The customer had a sore throat and could not speak, but he wrote "0.2 of the bar" on a piece of paper and gave it to Carl. How many pieces of chocolate should Carl give the man?

Mixed Numbers and Decimals

Jumping Jane just got the results of her latest two-toed broad jump. She jumped $5\frac{3}{10}$ ft. Her previous jumps were 5.5 ft, 5.1 ft, and 3.5 ft. Is this her best jump yet?

67 Fractions and Decimal Equivalents

Brainy Brian saw that his sister, Savant Sue, was taking an artichoke pie out of the oven. Brian said, "That looks great. Tell you what. If you give me 0.75 of it, we'll forget all about the $5 you owe me."

"Well," said Sue. "How about if I give you $\frac{3}{8}$ of it instead?" Which is a better deal for Brian?

68 Comparing and Ordering Decimals

Ignatius Icenoff is a Russian skating sensation. In his latest competition, the four judges gave him these final scores: France—9.80, USA—9.6, Germany—8.7, Canada—9.75. Who gave Ignatius the lowest score? Who gave him the highest score?

Comparing Fractions, Mixed Numbers, and Decimals

At the Annual Cheese-Lovers Convention, Connie Muenster saw a stand selling her all-time favorite—Stinkmeister Cheese. Connie wanted to buy as much as she could. There were four pre-wrapped packages already weighed and marked like this: 1.4 lbs, $1\frac{9}{10}$ lbs, 1.05 lbs, and $1\frac{15}{100}$ lbs. Which one should she buy to get the most cheese?

Adding and Subtracting Decimals

The countries of Snarksylvania and Rumplelonia are considering merging. Snarksylvania has a population of 8.2 million people. Rumplelonia has 1.7 million people. If Snarksylvania and Rumplelonia do merge, they will name the new country "Snarksylrumpia." How many people will there be in Snarksylrumpia if the merger goes through?

71 Adding and Subtracting Decimals

Marvin Munchenuff bought a 5.5-ounce bag of Creamy Ranch Crunchitos. His little brother, Milton, got to the bag first and ate 0.65 ounces of the tasty treats. How much of the Creamy Ranch Crunchitos were left?

72 Rounding Decimals

Gina Gamester was playing her favorite electronic game, Flying Electric Rat Chase. When she finished the game she announced, "I scored about 90 points!"

Her sister, Gemma, looked at the display and said, "No way! You scored only about 80 points!" The game display showed the number 88.80. Who was right—Gina or Gemma?

MEASUREMENT

73 — Inch, Half Inch, and Quarter Inch

Samantha's snake, Little Cuddles, is a quarter-inch longer than Beth's snake, Bacon Bit. Beth's snake is half an inch longer than Cynthia's snake, Floyd. Cynthia's snake is $8\frac{1}{2}$ inches long. How long is Little Cuddles?

74 — Perimeter

Roscoe Raccoon loves bowling. He wants his own bowling alley and he is going to build one underground. He wants it to be a rectangular shape, 85 feet long and 25 feet wide. What will the perimeter of his bowling alley be?

 **Capacity: Quarts/Pints/Gallons**

Doctor Dangerous is mixing his special serum again. He makes 8 quarts* of the stuff at a time. He usually gives his "friends" a cup each. How many friends can he serve with the batch he just made?

* 1 quart = 2 pints; 1 pint = 2 cups

 **Capacity: Quarts/Pints/Gallons**

Sixteen quarts* is a lot of Venusian salad dressing, but that's what Amy ordered. It arrives in one big tub. She wants to sell it in gallon containers. How many gallon containers will she need?

* 4 quarts = 1 gallon

77 Capacity: Ounces/Pounds/Tons

"Pimplelonium! The rarest of metals! I stuck it rich!" Klondike Katie was excited. "I just weighed it out and I got 64 ounces* out of my mine."

Her partner, Millie Miner said, "That's great, Kate! I've got a pound here myself. We can get $100 a pound at the precious metals exchange!" How much will the partners get paid in all?

* 16 ounces = 1 pound

78 Length: Centimeter and Meter

Cinderella's fairy godmother went to the Fairy Godmother Sewing Shop. "I need 280 cm* of lace trim for this sash I'm making for Cindy," she said.

The surly clerk replied, "We only sell it in meters, dearie." How many meters (to the nearest whole meter) of lace trim should Cinderella's fairy godmother ask for?

* 100 centimeters = 1 meter

79   Length: Meters and Kilometers

"I'm ready for the race. My new electric scooter goes 5 kilometers* an hour," Speedy said.

   "That's cool," replied his friend, Flash. "But, the race course you're going to be on is 5,000 meters long. How long will it take you to cover that, dude?" What should Speedy say?

* 1 kilometer = 1,000 meters

80   Metric Units of Capacity and Mass

It was going to be a hot day for the championship dinosaur chase. Cave girl Ug wanted to bring as much water as she could with her. Her mother said, "Well, the blue sport bottle holds 1 liter* and the green one holds 1,200 milliliters. Which one do you want?" What should Ug tell her mother? Why?

* 1 liter = 1,000 milliliters

81 Metric Units of Capacity and Mass

Roscoe wanted to bring his average-sized dog Peaches with him on vacation. The airline attendant who took care of pets had to weigh Peaches on the scale. "About 10," he called out. Do you think he meant 10 grams, 10 ounces, or 10 kilograms? Why?

82 Degrees Fahrenheit and Negative Numbers

The folks in Crankyville said it was colder there than anywhere else in the state on Wednesday. The temperature in Crankyville was 3° Fahrenheit. The folks in Bee City disagreed. The temperature there was –3° Fahrenheit. How much colder was it in Bee City than in Crankyville?

83 Degrees Celsius and Negative Numbers

In the Republic of Freezepopolonia they use Celsius thermometers to measure temperature. The temperature at noon was 10° Celsius, but by 3:00 P.M. the temperature had dropped 2°. By 9:00 P.M. it had dropped another 16°. What was the temperature at 9:00 P.M.?

84 Mean, Median, Mode

Coach Yelltoomuch is coach of a new team in the league, The Mighty Goldfish. He was looking over his basketball team's scoring from their first game. His chart looked like this:

1. Grumpy   12 points
2. Doc   13 points
3. Sleepy   14 points
4. Wheezy   12 points

5. Slippery   11 points
6. Slinky   13 points
7. Sloppy   23 points

The manager asked Coach Y for a full report on the Goldfish's offense. Prepare Coach's report for the manager. Order the data from least to greatest. Find the range, mode, median, and mean. Then identify any outliers.

85   Bar Graphs

Lots of snacks were sold at Junior's Snack Food Emporium. Here's a graph of the first year's results. Gumbo Yumbos and Flaming Purple Peanuts were both good sellers, but which of the two sold more? How much more?

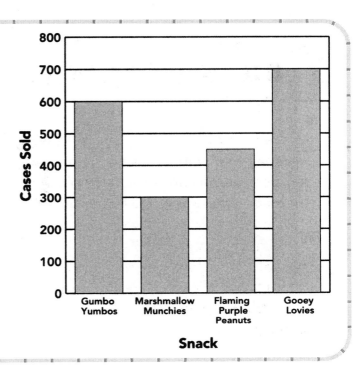

86   Line Graphs

A strange intergalactic plant was found growing behind the Happy Monkeys Preschool. It was growing so fast that the kids decided to measure it and create a line graph. Here's what it looked like. How tall was the plant after three days? On which day do you think the class forgot to water the plant?

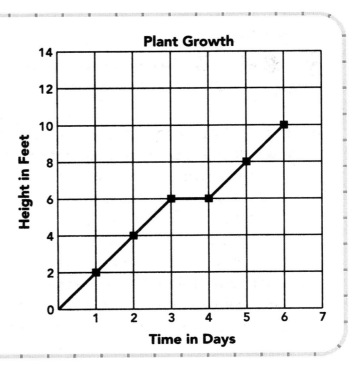

87 Probability and Outcomes

Marbella ordered a bag of mixed wing nuts. In the bag there were 8 green wing nuts and 2 red wing nuts. Use these words to describe the probability of picking certain wing nuts out of the bag on the first try: *likely, unlikely, certain, impossible.*

    a. red
    b. green
    c. purple
    d. red or green

88 Making Predictions

Gooey Greg's Gaming Emporium specializes in different games of chance. One game featured a box with 6 cards in it. The cards were 2 aces, a king, a queen, a jack, and a joker. You reached in the box and picked out a card. If you picked an ace you won. If you didn't, you lost. At the end of your turn your picked card went back in the box and the game would begin again. Lucky Larry played the game 600 times. He kind of liked it. About how many times would you predict he picked an ace?

89 Polygons and Quadrilaterals

Doctor Shapey was trying to complete his museum's new display—Scintillating Shapes. The only shape he is missing is a rectangle. A shape dealer offered him a pentagon, a triangle, or a square. Which one should he purchase for the display? Why?

90 Polygons and Quadrilaterals

On the famous "Guess Who I Am" television show a mysterious shape gave these clues while hiding behind the curtain: "I have more sides than a square, but less sides than a hexagon. I am a polygon." What was the name of the mystery shape?

91   Classify Triangles

Clyde was painting a cool design on his skateboard. On the top of his deck he painted a face that looked a lot like his principal but was shaped like a triangle with sides of 8 cm, 6 cm, and 8 cm. What kind of triangle did Clyde paint?

92   Perimeter and Area

Archie the architect was commissioned to design a new building honoring the achievements of cows. It's called, of course, the Mooseum. It's height is 90 feet. The base has two sides that are each 90 feet long and two other sides that are each 150 feet long. What is the perimeter of The Mooseum?

93 Perimeter and Area

The curators of the Mooseum are ready to move in the cow exhibits. They have exhibits that will cover 10,000 square feet of floor space. They told Archie when he designed the 90-ft-by-150-ft building to make sure there was at least that much floor space. The Mooseum is a one-story building. Is Archie in trouble? Why or why not?

94 Solid Figures

Archie the architect continued to create impressive buildings. His latest creation, the Hall of Crackers, is one huge triangular prism. How many triangles did he use?

95 Surface Area

Polly Perfection is wrapping a birthday present for her friend, Samantha Surfacearea. The box is a rectangular prism. It has a height of 2 inches, a length of 7 inches, and a width of 3 inches. How many square inches of wrapping paper does she need exactly to cover the box?

96 Volume

Salamandra is an unusual girl, but sweet. She likes to eat sugar cubes. Specifically those that are one square cm. She was putting them in boxes that are 2 cm high, 3 cm wide, and 4 cm long. How many cubes could she fit in 3 boxes?

97 Integers

Big Spender Basil started the day with $100 in his checking account. Using his new checks, he bought a hot pretzel with avocado sauce for $3. He also bought a parakeet who could do algebra for $20. Finally he bought an $80 folding yo-yo cleaner. What integer could be used to represent his final checking account balance?

$$2x + y = 36$$

98 Missing Addend

Marvin started his new job in the widget factory. He put 9,325 widgets in the widget organizing tray. Marvin could not move the tray until all 9,500 compartments were filled. How many more widgets did he need to fill the tray?

Algebra/Surface Area

The wonderful new Tower of Taste is being made of pure chocolate cubes stacked one on the top of the other. Each cube has a 5-ft-by-5-ft face. There are 4 cubes so far on the tower. What is its surface area?

Algebra/Properties

Wondrous Willy was working on his garden while his sister Willa watched nearby. He said, "I've got 24 rows of beets and there are 32 beets in a row. I wonder how many beets that is? Probably the easiest way to do this is to multiply 20 x 30 and then multiply 4 x 2, and add the results together. What do you think Willa?"

"Beets me," said Willa. What should Willa say?

ANSWER KEY

Place Value and Number

1. Skunkfoot Stadium

2. 400,000 nose rings

3. 17 points

4. 5 boxes

5. About 1,200 points a month

6. 987,654,321 or nine hundred eighty-seven million, six hundred fifty-four thousand, three hundred twenty-one

7. Yes

8. About 11 million

9. Mr. Yawn; $11.05

10. One $5 bill, three $1 bills, a dime, and two pennies

11. A $5 bill; $1.35 + $3.65 = $5.00

Addition and Subtraction

12. 915 noodles

13. 89 children signed up for archery and 89 children signed up for ping-pong.

14. 183 children signed up for Count Factula's camp; 183 children signed up for Mr. Hyden's camp

15. 15,000 books

16. 38,840 pieces of gum

17. 6,049 whistles

18. 8,557 more crazy wigs

19. Yes. If you round up $3.89 to the nearest dime you get $3.90, and if you round up $1.49 you get $1.50. $3.90 + $1.50 = $5.40.

20. About 170 Ookie-Man cards

21. 1,510 gizzies

Multiplication and Division

22. 128 books

23. $68

24. Both boys had the same amount of rocks on display. 8 x 9 = 72 and 9 x 8 = 72

25. 121 minutes

26. 24 cereal boxes

27. Yes. 9 x 10 = 90 hot dogs, and only 83 students are coming.

28. 9 teams; 9 x 3 = 27

29. 24 gift boxes

30. 5 fellas in each boat

31. 8 stickers

32. 6 people

33. 6 container ships

34. 8 sling shots; he will have 3 extra pebbles in his pocket

35. Yes. She climbed 1,600 feet.

36. 9 boxes

37. $40,000

38. Penelope

39. 144 doughnuts

40. About 1,050 minutes

41. 642 weeds

42. No. He'll have 10,344 bottle caps already.

43. $14.70

44. 3,204

45. Hermione

46. No. $18 ÷ 3 = $6

47. Each club got 22 bikes; the police got 2 bikes.

48. 12 pages for each school day left; 2 pages during summer vacation

49. 50 cards

50. 124 planets

51. $1.12

52. 208 points

53. 5 ringers

54. 25 tickets

55. 1,555 marshmallows at each station; there were no extras to eat

Fractions and Mixed Numbers

56. $\frac{7}{12}$

57. 14 lunch tickets

58. They each have the same number of boys.

59. Yes. $\frac{12}{18}$ is the same as $\frac{2}{3}$ and the measuring cup has thirds on it.

60. Crew #1 got more painting done. $\frac{4}{12}$ is the same as $\frac{1}{3}$, and $\frac{2}{3}$ is more than $\frac{1}{3}$.

61. $2\frac{3}{4}$ waffles

62. $\frac{7}{8}$ of a yard

63. $2\frac{5}{10}$ or $2\frac{1}{2}$ gold bricks

64. $0.75; that's more than $\frac{7}{10}$ of a dollar, which is $0.70.

65. 40 pieces

66. No; 5.5 ft is her best jump.

67. 0.75 of the pie

68. Germany gave him the lowest score; France gave him the highest score.

69. $1\frac{9}{10}$ lbs

70. 9.9 million people

71. 4.85 ounces

72. Gina

Measurement

73. $9\frac{1}{4}$ inches long

74. 220 feet

75. 32 friends

76. 4 gallon containers

77. $500

78. 3 meters

79. 1 hour

80. She should ask for the green bottle because 1,200 milliliters is more than 1 liter.

81. About 10 kilograms, because 10 grams or 10 ounces would be too light for an average-sized dog.

82. 6 degrees colder

83. −8° Celsius

Data Analysis and Probability

84. Range—12
Mode—12, 13
Median—13
Mean—14
Outliers—23

85. Gumbo Yumbos sold 150 more cases

86. 6 feet; they forgot to water the plant on day 3

87. a. unlikely
b. likely
c. impossible
d. certain

88. About 200 times

Geometry

89. The square, because a square is a type of rectangle

90. Pentagon

91. Isosceles

92. 480 feet

93. No. His building has 13,500 square feet of floor space.

94. 2 triangles

95. 82 square inches

96. 72 cubes

Algebra

97. –$3

98. 175 widgets

99. 450 square feet

100. That would not work because 20 x 30 = 600 and 4 x 2 = 8. Added together that would be 608. The correct answer is 768 beets.

TEACHER'S NOTES